Successes That Happened without Any Effort

Karl W. Palachuk

Published by the Humor Department of

Great Little Book Publishing Co.
Sacramento, CA

Successes That Happened without Any Effort.

ISBN: 978-1-942115-16-8

Note:

This is a **blank gift book**, intended to bring joy into your life. Feel free to fill the inside pages with your own thoughts and jokes.

If you would like to find more Blank books – or create your own as a gift – visit **www.BlankGiftBook.com**.

Blank Gift Books make great presents for birthdays, anniversaries, Christmas, Mother's Day, or any other occasion.

Successes That Happened without Any Effort

The Real Story:

Nothing Happens by Itself!
— Karl W. Palachuk

When you're ready to start working on your amazing future, start by reading (or listening to):

Notes:

_____

_____

_____

_____

_____

_____

_____

_____

_____

More Titles in This Series . . .
From BlankGiftBook.com

What You Should Expect from Your Ex-Wife
by Mia Culpa

The Big Guide to Honest Politicians
by Pat McCann

How to Make Women Feel Better During Menopause
by Les Moody

How to Be an Attorney and Keep Your Soul
by Sue First

The Complete Guide to Humility for MDs
by Anita Procedure

How to Find Job Security in Corporate America
by Justin Case

What Men Know About Making Women Feel Special
by Mike Easter

… And you can even create your own Blank Gift Book at

www.BlankGiftBook.com